A Mess

by Jan Stewart
illustrated by Anni Matsick

Core Decodable 63

Bothell, WA • Chicago, IL • Columbus, OH • New York, NY

MHEonline.com

Copyright © 2015 McGraw-Hill Education

All rights reserved. No part of this publication may be reproduced or distributed in any form or by any means, or stored in a database or retrieval system, without the prior written consent of McGraw-Hill Education, including, but not limited to, network storage or transmission, or broadcast for distance learning.

Send all inquiries to:
McGraw-Hill Education
8787 Orion Place
Columbus, OH 43240

ISBN: 978-0-02-144995-8
MHID: 0-02-144995-3

Printed in the United States of America.

2 3 4 5 6 7 8 9 DOC 20 19 18 17 16 15

The park is a mess!
It is time to pick up.

What trash did we find?
Well, we see a bike tire!

This wide bag is mine.
I filled it with paper.

This is a smashed kite.
This is a plastic pipe.

We picked up a lot.
We made a big junk pile.

We can ride bikes in the park.
Hikers can walk on a path.